Tapi Appreciates MOMS

BOOK 2

The Little Moments of Motherhood

by MommyHooray

Motherhood is steady work filled with purpose.
Every loving choice helps guide a growing heart.
Its impact reaches far beyond the day.

Tapi Appreciates Moms
by MommyHooray

Written and published under the pen name MommyHooray.
Illustrations created using digital illustration tools.

Printed in the United States of America.

ISBN: 978-1-972071-21-2

For more stories and updates, visit:
https://sites.google.com/view/mommyhooray/

This book is dedicated
to all the extraordinary moms
who give so much,
often quietly and without pause.
Thank you for your love, your care,
and your endless devotion.
You are deeply appreciated.

With Googolplex Love,

For moms who carry more than seen,
Between the loud and in-between.
For steady hands and watchful eyes,
For love that never asks us why.
In every role, in every place,
You meet the world with honest grace.
This book begins with thanks so true,
For all the love that comes from you.

MORNING-RUSH MOM

Before the day even finds its pace,
You're already winning the morning race.

CARPOOL MOM

Seatbelts click, the playlist repeats,
You practically live on familiar streets.

WORKING MOM

You balance hours, hearts, and space,
Making time bend to your pace.

STAY-AT-HOME MOM

You sit for a minute—then hear a call,
Rest postponed by “Mom?” down the hall.

NIGHT-SHIFT MOM

As others sleep and stars drift by,
Your love stays awake through the night sky.

EARLY-RISER MOM

Before the light even learns to glow,
You rise for needs the world won't know.

LATE-NIGHT MOM

When quiet finally fills the air,
You finish the things left waiting there.

SPORTY MOM

With claps and cheers you never miss,
Your steady presence feels like bliss.

HOMEWORK MOM

Numbers tangle, questions climb,
You offer calm one step at a time.

SNACK-PACKING MOM

Snacks at hand, just in case,
Love shows up in every place.

BEDTIME-ROUTINE MOM

With whispered words and gentle tone,
You guide them safely toward their own.

LAUNDRY-DAY MOM

Wash, fold, stack, then repeat,
Love lives in each quiet beat.

ERRAND-RUNNING MOM

Between the lists and places run,
You find small joys till chores are done.

APPOINTMENT MOM

Dates and times you neatly thread,
Every detail stored in your head.

AFTER-SCHOOL MOM

With open arms and something more,
You catch their day right at the door.

CALENDAR-KEEPING MOM

You remember what slips their mind,
Living three weeks ahead in time.

BUDGETING MOM

You stretch each dollar, calm and slow,
Performing math no one will know.

MEAL-PLANNING MOM

You plan ahead with loving care,
So every mealtime's always there.

CLEAN-UP MOM

With patient hands, the chaos bends,
And order finds its way again.

SICK-DAY MOM

Plans dissolve without a sound,
Presence is where you are found.

FIELD–TRIP MOM

Forms signed fast, no detail tripped,
You show up steady, ready, equipped.

WAITING-IN-THE-CAR MOM

Between the stop and what comes next,
You calm the wait with gentle text.

WEEKEND-SHIFT MOM

Different hours, same deep care,
Love doesn't clock out anywhere.

PHONE-CALL MOM

Between each ring, you calmly steer,
A thousand answers sharp and clear.

MY MOM

Your love became my inner voice,
Guiding me through every choice.

From moms before us, strong and kind,
To moms who shape the next in line.
Your care moves on from day to day,
A gift that time can't take away.
Though words may fade and pages close,
Your love remains in all it grows.
A mother's heart, both fierce and true,
Keeps living on in all we do.

From My Heart to Yours

Write a note, memory, or wish for the person who will treasure this book.

Today's Date: ____________________

May this page find you again, years from now.

www.ingramcontent.com/pod-product-compliance
Lightning Source LLC
LaVergne TN
LVHW070204110826
845147LV00002B/493